The Seven Brothers and the Big Dipper

북두칠성이 된 형제들

Hungbu, Nolbu and the Magic Gourds

흥부와 놀부

 HOLLYM

The Seven Brothers and the Big Dipper

Every night, we can see countless stars in the sky twinkling. This story is about a group of seven stars we call the Big Dipper.

A long time ago, in a small village there lived an old lady with her seven sons. They were very poor, but even so they all lived together very happily.

The seven brothers grew up very fast and were soon able to help their mother with her chores.

북두칠성이 된 형제들

밤 하늘에는 셀 수 없이 많은 별들이 반짝이고 있습니다.

그 가운데 옹기종기 모여 있는 일곱 개의 별에 대한 이야기입니다.

옛날 어느 마을에 홀어머니와 아들 일곱 형제가 살고 있었습니다.

비록 가난했지만, 여덟 식구는 오순 도순 행복하게 살았습니다.

일곱 형제는 어느덧 무럭무럭 자라 어머니의 일손을 덜어 주었습니다.

One year, in the early winter, the children got together and decided, "This winter, let's gather up lots of firewood so that Mother can stay warm."

The seven brothers stacked a large pile of wood in the yard. Everyday, they made a fire with the wood to keep their mother's room warm. Even so, their mother always looked like she was cold.

The seven brothers became worried and so they asked her, "Mother, there anything we can do to make you feel better?"

"I don't feel very well now," she said, "but I'll be okay. Don't worry."

But the seven brothers could hear her inside the warm room at night muttering to herself, "Oh, I am so cold."

어느 해 이른 겨울이었습니다.
"올 겨울도 어머니가 따뜻하게 지내시도록 해드리자."
일곱 형제는 뒤뜰에 장작을 가득히 쌓아 놓고 날마다 어머니 방에 군불을 지펴드렸습니다.
그러나 어머니는 늘 추운 얼굴을 하고 지냈습니다.

"어머니 어디 편찮은 데라도 있으세요?"
아들들이 걱정이 되어 물었습니다.
"아니 아프긴, 괜찮다. 걱정 말아라."
어머니는 이렇게 말했지만, 따뜻한 방에서도 곧잘 '아휴 추워' 하고 혼잣말을 했습니다.

One night, the oldest brother woke up and saw that his mother's bed was empty. He thought to himself, "How strange. Where could Mother be in the middle of the night?" He was so worried he stayed awake in his bed at night, waiting for his mother to return.

Finally, she came in quietly, just before dawn.

The oldest brother wondered, "Where could she go when it's so cold outside?"

So the next night, he only pretended to be asleep so he could watch his mother.

어느 날 밤이었습니다.

큰아들이 잠에서 깨어 일어나보니 방 안에 어머니가 없었습니다.

'이상하다. 어머니가 이 밤중에 어딜 가신 걸까?'

큰아들은 걱정이 되어 어머니를 기다렸습니다.

큰아들은 다음 날 밤 일부러 자는 체하고 누워 어머니를 지켜 보았습니다.

The night grew deeper. When it was very late, she quietly got up. Looking to see if her sons were sleeping, she tiptoed out of the room.

The oldest brother followed his mother as quietly as he could. She went outside the village and came to a small creek that had a thin layer of ice on it. She paused for just a moment and then splashed across the creek. "Oh! This is so cold," she sighed, as she walked through the ice-cold water.

After she crossed the stream, Mother kept going until she reached a small, out-of-the-way hut.

밤이 점점 깊어갔습니다.

어머니는 살그머니 일어나 발자국 소리도 없이 밖으로 나갔습니다.

큰아들은 조용히 따라 일어나 가만가만 어머니의 뒤를 밟았습니다.

어머니는 어느새 동구밖을 지나 조그만 시냇가에 다다랐습니다.

잠시 머뭇거리던 어머니는 살얼음이 낀 냇물을 철벅철벅 건너기 시작했습니다.

"아유, 차가와라."

냇물을 다 건넌 어머니는 외딴 오두막집 앞에서 발을 멈추었습니다.

"Hello. Are you here?" Mother whispered softly at the door. An old gentleman came out right away and greeted her warmly. The oldest brother tiptoed up to the house and peeked through a crack in the door. His mother and the old gentleman took turns scratching each other's back while they talked together quietly. They seemed to enjoy talking very much.

"Mother has been very lonely. I guess she needs a friend to talk to."

The oldest brother finally nodded his head in understanding.

"여보세요, 안 계세요?"
어머니는 나직이 누군가를 불렀습니다.

그러자 집 안에서 영감 한 사람이 나와 어머니를 반가이 맞아들였습니다.

큰아들은 살금살금 다가가서 문틈으로 빼꼼이 방안을 엿보았습니다.

두 사람은 서로 등을 긁어 주면서 두런두런 재미있게 이야기를 나누고 있었습니다.

'어머니가 무척 외로우셨구나. 어머니는 말동무가 필요하셨어.'

큰아들은 비로소 고개를 끄덕였습니다.

13

So the oldest brother waded back across the creek and quickly returned home. He woke his brothers up and told them, "Mother has been so cold because every night she wades across an icy creek to go to the old shoemaker's house. It seems like she needs a friend she can talk to."

One of the brothers spoke up. "Then, let's make a bridge across the creek." The oldest brother agreed, saying, "Yes. Let's do that ! "

So all seven brothers ran to the creek. "Heave ho ! Heave ho ! " they shouted as they pulled big stones to the creek. Then they put stepping stones all the way across the stream.

큰아들은 첨벙첨벙 냇물을 건너 단숨에 집으로 돌아왔습니다.

그리고 자고 있는 동생들을 깨웠습니다.

"얘들아, 어머니가 추워하시는 건 밤마다 차가운 냇물을 건너시기 때문이란다. 어머니는 매일 밤 짚신 삼는 영감님 댁에 말동무를 하러 다녀오신단다."

"형님, 우리가 그 냇물에 다리를 놓아드려요."

"그래, 빨리 다리를 놓자."

형제들은 곧 냇물로 달려나갔습니다.

"영차 영차……."

일곱 형제는 큰 돌을 날라다가 징검다리를 놓았습니다.

Dawn came and Mother started her homeward journey. But when she came to the creek and saw the stone walkway, she exclaimed in astonishment, "Oh, my! Isn't that nice! I wonder who built such a fine bridge across the creek during the night."

She looked up at the sky and prayed. "Oh, Lord. Whoever has built this bridge, please make them stars in your heaven."

The seven brothers lived very happy lives. And when they died, many years later, they became the seven stars of the Big Dipper.

People could look up at those stars and tell which direction was north, since the oldest brother in the big dipper was the Pole Star. And people could even measure time by looking at the way the other six stars changed their position in the night sky.

흰하게 동이 터 왔습니다.

집으로 돌아오던 어머니는 냇물에 놓인 징검다리를 보고 깜짝 놀랐습니다.

"어머나, 고맙기도 해라. 누가 다리를 놓았을까?"

어머니는 하늘을 향해 기도했습니다.

"하느님, 이 다리를 놓아 준 사람은 하늘의 별이 되게 해 주세요."

그 후 행복하게 잘 살다가 죽은 착한 일곱 형제는 북두칠성이라는 일곱 개의 별이 되었습니다.

큰형은 국자모양 별자리의 손잡이가 되어, 북두칠성을 바라보는 사람들에게 많은 도움을 주었습니다. 사람들은 밤하늘에서 자리를 옮겨가는 북두칠성을 보고 시간을 재었습니다.

Hungbu, Nolbu and the Magic Gourds

A long time ago, in a village in Korea, there lived a mean boy called Nolbu. Wherever Nolbu went, people would shake their heads in disgust.

One day, his father couldn't stand it any longer. He gave Nolbu a severe scolding. He said, "Nolbu! Why are you such a trouble-maker? You stuck a stick in the green pumpkin. You hit a little boy and made him cry. You chased the chickens and scared the cows. The next time you act mean, I will kick you out of the house!"

흥부와 놀부

옛날, 전라도 어느 마을에 놀부라는 심술이 사나운 아이가 있었습니다.

마을 사람들은 놀부가 옆을 지나가면 설레설레 머리를 흔들며 피하곤 했습니다.

어느 날, 놀부의 아버지는 참다 못해 아들을 호되게 꾸짖었습니다.

"놀부야, 넌 왜 말썽만 부리느냐! 애호박에 말뚝 박고, 똥 누는 놈 주저앉히고, 우는 아이 더 때리고······. 또 한번 말썽을 부리면 집 밖으로 내쫓을 줄 알아라."

Nolbu had a younger brother called Hungbu. The two were as unlike as they could be. While Nolbu was mean, Hungbu was very goodhearted.

As the years passed, the two brothers grew up and got married. Then their mother died and their father fell ill.

"I know I will not live much longer. After I die, take everything I own and divide it equally into two portions and live well together."

But as soon as he had finished saying this, he took his last breath.

Nolbu did not seem very sad. He acted like he had been waiting for this moment for a very long time. He took all of his father's things for himself instead of sharing with Hungbu.

심술꾸러기 놀부에게는 흥부라는 동생이 있었는데, 형과는 달리 마음씨가 아주 고왔습니다.

세월이 흘러 두 형제는 장성하여 결혼도 하였습니다. 흥부와 놀부의 어머니가 돌아가시고, 아버지마저 병들어 누웠습니다.

어느 날, 아버지가 말했습니다.

"애들아, 나는 아무래도 더 못 살겠구나. 둘이서 재산을 반으로 나누어 가지고 함께 잘 살아라."

아버지는 이렇게 말을 남기고 곧 숨을 거두었습니다.

놀부는 전혀 슬퍼 보이지 않았습니다. 아버지가 돌아가시자 기다렸다는 듯이 모든 재산을 혼자 차지했습니다.

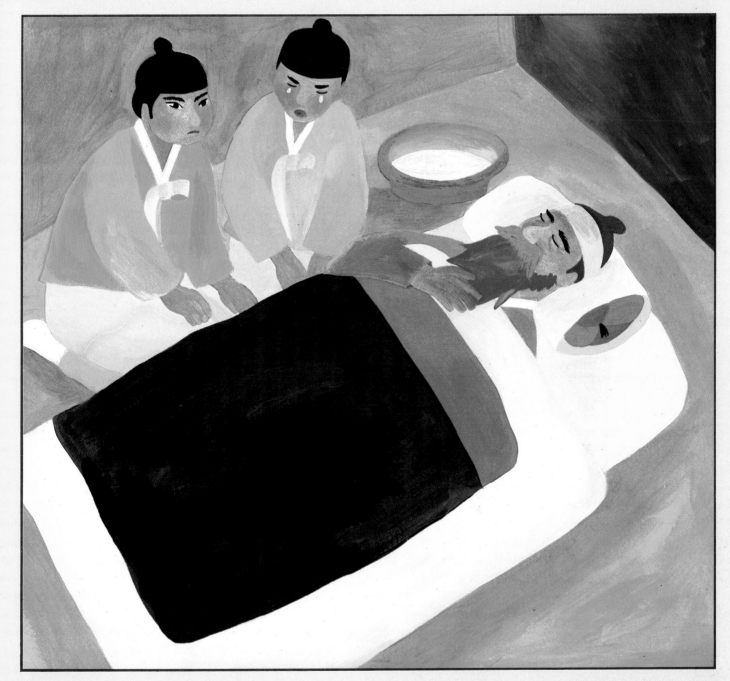

21

So, left with nothing, Hungbu and his family had to live and work in Nolbu's house to survive.

Then one day, Nolbu's wife, who was almost as mean as Nolbu, said to Nolbu, "Hungbu and his family will cause us to starve to death! They eat so much that there's never anything left."

"Is that so?" said Nolbu. "I'll just have to kick them out of the house."

So he called Hungbu and told him in a loud voice, "You stupid fool, I can't put up with your bothering my family any longer. Get out of my house at once!"

So, for no reason at all, Nolbu made poor Hungbu and his family go away.

흥부네 식구는 놀부네 집에서 일을 해주며 어렵게 살았습니다.

그러던 어느 날, 마음씨 나쁜 놀부의 아내가 놀부에게 말했습니다.

"여보, 우리는 흥부네 식구들 때문에 굶어 죽겠어요. 애들이 얼마나 먹어 대는지 음식이 남아나질 않아요."

"그래? 그렇다면 당장 쫓아내야지."

놀부는 큰 소리로 흥부를 불렀습니다.

"이 놈 흥부야, 너희 식구들 등쌀에 더 이상 못 견디겠으니 당장 내 집을 나가거라."

놀부는 다짜고짜 흥부를 내쫓았습니다.

22

Penniless and homeless, Hungbu's family wandered here and there for a long time, working when and where they could. Finally, they were able to build a very small hut at the foot of the mountain.

But they knew a very cold winter was coming, and they had run out of food. After much thought, Hungbu's wife said to him, "Could you please go to your brother and try to get something for us to eat. Even a little barley would help."

홍부네 식구는 빈털터리로 쫓겨났습니다.

여기저기를 헤매던 홍부네 식구는 산기슭으로 올라가 조그만 오두막을 지었습니다.

홍부와 아내는 이집 저집을 돌아다니며 열심히 일했습니다.

그러나 곧 추운 겨울이 닥쳐오고 먹을 것이 다 떨어져 버렸습니다.

홍부의 아내는 궁리 끝에 홍부에게 말했습니다.

"여보 형님댁에 가서 보리쌀이라도 좀 얻어오세요."

Hungbu had more concern for his hungry family than he had for his own pride, so he went to Nolbu's house. "Older Brother, could you please spare a few cups of barley?" he asked.

But Nolbu turned red with anger. "What! A young healthy man like you begging for something to eat? What a lazy bum you are!" he shouted and drove Hungbu away with a stick.

As he was running out of the house, Hungbu happened to look into the kitchen and saw Nolbu's wife dishing out from the rice pot a steaming ladle of hot rice.

흥부는 배가 고파서 휘청거리며 놀부를 찾아갔습니다.

"형님, 보리쌀 몇 되만 꾸어 주세요."
그러자 놀부는 벌컥 화를 냈습니다.
"아니, 젊은 놈이 남의 집에 쌀이나 꾸러 다녀? 이런 게으른 놈 같으니라구!"

놀부는 몽둥이를 휘두르며 흥부를 내쫓았습니다.

허겁지겁 쫓겨나던 흥부는 부엌에 있는 놀부의 아내를 보았습니다.

마침 놀부의 아내는 김이 술술 나는 밥을 주걱으로 푸고 있었습니다.

27

"Dear sister-in-law," he called to her, "Please spare me just one spoonful of rice to take home."

But as soon as she saw him, sister-in-law gave him a mean look. Then she picked up the flat wooden spoon she had been using to dish out the rice and hit Hungbu smack on the cheek with it. Some of the rice from the spatula stuck to Hungbu's cheek. He quickly pulled the grains of rice from his cheek and ate them saying, "My sister-in-law gives me rice when she hits me. Sister-in-law, could you please hit me again and again so I can take some rice home to my hungry family?"

This made her madder. So she very carefully washed the rice off the wooden spatula, and then she hit Hungbu's face again with all her strength.

"형수님, 밥 한 술만 주십쇼."

놀부의 아내는 흥부를 보자마자 눈을 치켜떴습니다.

그러더니 밥을 푸던 주걱으로 흥부의 뺨을 철썩 갈겼습니다.

"형수님은 밥을 붙여 주면서 때리시는군요."

흥부는 뺨을 어루만지면서 얼굴에 붙은 밥알을 떼어 먹었습니다.

"형수님 이쪽 뺨도 마저 때려 주십쇼."

흥부가 이렇게 말하자, 약이 오른 놀부의 아내는 주걱의 밥알을 싹싹 닦아 낸 뒤 또다시 흥부의 뺨을 냅다 갈겼습니다.

Spring came.

Hungbu's family had somehow managed to make it through the winter. A pair of swallows came to Hungbu's house and built a nest.

Before long some cute little swallows hatched.

But one day, when Hungbu came home from work, he saw a big snake slithering around the swallows' nest. He quickly grabbed a stick and drove the snake away. But he was too late. The snake had eaten all of the baby birds, except for one which had fallen to the ground when it tried to escape.

"Oh, the poor little bird has broken its leg," Hungbu said sadly. He carefully bound the baby swallow's leg with some leather string and put it back in its nest.

봄이 왔습니다.

어렵게 겨울을 난 홍부의 집에도 제비 한 쌍이 날아와 집을 지었습니다.

얼마 지나자, 귀여운 새끼제비들이 알에서 깨어났습니다.

그런데 어느 날 홍부가 일을 마치고 돌아와보니, 커다란 구렁이가 제비집 속에 머리를 들이밀고 있었습니다.

홍부는 얼른 막대기를 가져다가 구렁이를 내쫓아 버렸습니다.

새끼제비들은 다 잡아 먹히고, 한 마리만 뜰아래에 떨어져 있었습니다.

"쯧쯧, 어린 것이 다리가 부러졌구나!"

홍부는 새끼제비의 다리를 헝겊으로 잘 매어서 둥지에 올려 주었습니다.

After its leg healed, the baby bird grew up strong and healthy. When winter came, along with the other birds, it flew south for the winter. But the following spring, it came back to Hungbu's house. It circled the small yard. Then it landed and dropped at Hungbu's feet a tiny gourd seed that it was carrying in its beak.

Hungbu and his family planted the gourd seed carefully beside their house.

Soon, autumn came again. On top of Hungbu's roof, three giant gourds hung in clusters from a single vine. One day, Hungbu cut the gourds from the vine and called to his family to help cut them open so they could be cooked and eaten. As they worked, they sang a little song.

다리의 상처가 아물자, 새끼제비는 건강해졌습니다.

가을이 되자, 제비들은 겨울을 나러 따뜻한 남쪽 나라로 날아갔습니다.

이듬해 봄, 홍부네 집에는 제비 한 마리가 찾아왔습니다.

제비는 마당을 뱅뱅 돌다가 입에 물고 있던 박씨를 '툭' 떨어뜨리고 갔습니다.

홍부네 식구는 울 밑에 제비가 준 박씨를 잘 심었습니다.

이윽고 가을이 왔습니다.

홍부네 집 지붕 위에는 탐스러운 박들이 주렁주렁 열렸습니다. 어느 날, 홍부는 지붕 위에 박을 따 내렸습니다.

홍부네 식구들은 옹기종기 둘러앉아 박을 타기 시작했습니다.

"Cut, cut, let's cut this good gourd open.
Let's steam it and eat it.
Cut, cut, let's cut this good gourd open.
Let's boil it up and eat it."

Hungbu and his family laughed and sang as they sawed open the gourd. Then with a loud crack, the gourd broke in half. Hungbu's family was very surprised. All sorts of gold and jewelry spilled out from the gourd.

Then they cut open the second gourd. So much rice flowed out of the gourd that it filled their whole yard.

When they cut open the third gourd, all sorts of wood and bricks tumbled out. They used the wood and bricks to build a magnificent house with a tiled roof.

슬근슬근 톱질이야.
이 박 속은 지져 먹고,
슬근슬근 톱질이야.
이 박 속은 삶아 먹자.

흥부네 식구들은 장단도 흥겹게 박을 탔습니다.
'쫙'하고 박이 갈라졌습니다.

흥부네 식구들은 깜짝 놀랐습니다.
박 속에서 갖가지 금은 보화가 쏟아져 나온 것입니다.
둘째 박을 가르니 쌀이 쏟아져 나와 마당에 가득 쌓였습니다.
세째 박에서는 목수들이 우르르 나와 단숨에 으리으리한 기와집을 지었습니다.

Hungbu was suddenly a very rich man. When Nolbu heard his brother had become wealthy, he became very cross. Finally, when he couldn't stand it anymore, he set out to visit Hungbu's house. He saw the grand gate and the roof of the magnificent house. He knocked and Hungbu opened the gate and let him in.

"You must have stolen all this from somewhere to have gotten rich so fast! Tell me the truth now. How did you become so rich?" Nolbu said in astonishment.

"I didn't steal a thing," Hungbu said, and then he explained how he became rich.

While Nolbu listened to Hungbu's story, he picked up all of the small expensive things that he could sneak out in his clothes and headed back home.

흥부는 갑자기 큰 부자가 되었습니다.

이 소문을 들은 놀부는 심술이 나서 견딜 수가 없었습니다.

놀부는 부랴부랴 흥부를 찾아왔습니다.

으리으리한 집의 커다란 대문과 지붕을 보았습니다.

문을 두드리자, 흥부가 문을 열고 그를 안으로 안내했습니다.

"네 이놈, 흥부야! 어디서 도둑질을 해 왔기에 하룻밤 사이에 부자가 되었느냐! 어서 바른 대로 말하여라."

"저는 아무것도 훔치지 않았습니다."

흥부는 어떻게 부자가 되었는지를 설명해 주었습니다.

From that day on, Nolbu waited for a swallow to come to his house.

After another long winter, spring finally came. A pair of swallows came to Nolbu's house and built a nest under the eaves of the roof. After a while, several young birds hatched from their eggs.

Nolbu waited for a snake to come. But none ever did.

Finally, he couldn't wait any longer. He took a baby swallow from the nest and broke its leg. He then shouted at it, "Listen to me, little swallow. When you get big, you have to bring me a magic gourd seed." Then Nolbu carelessly wrapped up the swallow's broken leg and shoved the bird back into the nest.

놀부는 그날부터 제비들이 오기만을 기다렸습니다.

긴 겨울이 지나고, 드디어 봄이 왔습니다. 놀부네 집 처마 밑에도 제비 한 쌍이 날아와 집을 지었습니다.

얼마 뒤에 새끼제비들이 알을 깨고 나왔습니다.

놀부는 이제나저제나 구렁이가 오기를 기다렸습니다.

그러나 구렁이는 오지 않았습니다.

참다 못한 놀부는 둥지에 있는 새끼 제비를 끄집어내어 다리를 부러뜨렸습니다.

"제비야, 얼른 커서 박씨를 물어온."

놀부는 제비 다리를 아무렇게나 칭칭 묶어 주었습니다.

The swallow leg healed and later the bird flew south for the winter. The next spring, the swallow flew back to Nolbu's house, dropped two gourd seeds on the ground, and then flew away as quickly as it could.

Nolbu was overjoyed. He happily planted the two seeds.

The gourds grew and grew. As soon as the gourds were ripe, Nolbu and his wife started cutting them open.

"Cut, cut, let's cut the rich gourd open.

Come out gold, come out silver."

And the gourd split open with a loud crack.

As soon as it opened, hundreds of beggars came wiggling and wiggling and jiggling out of the gourd. Like a swarm of locust, in minutes the beggars had eaten every bit of food that was in Nolbu's house. And then they all disappeared.

놀부가 다리를 부러뜨린 새끼제비는 가을이 되어 남쪽 나라로 떠났습니다.

이듬해 봄, 제비는 놀부네 집으로 돌아와 박씨 한 개를 던져주고 갔습니다.

놀부는 신이 나서 박씨를 심었습니다. 박이 여물었습니다.

놀부와 아내는 서둘러 톱을 가져다가 박을 가르기 시작했습니다.

슬근슬근 톱질이야.

금 나오고, 은 나와라.

박이 쩍 갈라졌습니다.

그러자 박 속에서 수백 명의 거지들이 우글우글 쏟아져 나왔습니다.

거지들은 놀부네 집 음식을 닥치는 대로 먹어 치우고 사라졌습니다.

Nolbu cried out, "This can't be ! The gold must be in one of the other gourds."

As fast as he could, he cut open another gourd. But this time, instead of a gang of beggars, a horde of savage-looking men rushed out. They took all of Nolbu's money and valuables and disappeared.

"Oh, no !" cried Nolbu. "What can I do ? I am finished. Oh, what can I do ?"

And Nolbu got madder and madder. With tears in his eyes, he said, "I won't give up yet ! I know it's in the last gourd !"

And he cut open the final gourd without another thought.

But when the gourd fell open, a dreadful monster came out and beat Nolbu and his wife with a big iron club.

"이럴 리가 없어. 다른 박에서는 금이 나올 거야."

놀부는 허둥지둥 다른 박을 탔습니다.

그러자 이번에는 험상궂은 사람들이 우르르 나와 놀부의 돈과 보물을 모두 빼앗아 갔습니다.

"아이고, 나는 망했다. 아이고……."

놀부는 분해서 울다가 '이번에는 틀림없겠지' 하면서 남은 박을 탔습니다.

그런데 박이 갈라지자, 무시무시한 도깨비가 나와 쇠방망이로 놀부와 아내를 마구 때렸습니다.

Then the monster destroyed Nolbu's house and all of his belongings before it disappeared forever.

When Hungbu and his wife came running up to see what was the matter, Nolbu and his wife were lying on the ground, completely out of their senses.

Hungbu splashed some water on Nolbu's face to wake him up. Nolbu opened his swollen eyes with great difficulty. He looked at Hungbu with tears in his eyes and told him, "Hungbu, I was wrong." And Hungbu said, "Brother, you may come and live with us."

After that, Hungbu and Nolbu got along so well together that they were the envy of the whole village.

도깨비는 집과 살림을 모두 부수고 어디론가 사라져 버렸습니다.

놀부와 아내는 정신을 잃고 쓰러져 있었습니다.

그 때 흥부네 식구들이 달려왔습니다.

흥부는 놀부에게 물을 먹여 깨어나게 했습니다.

놀부는 가까스로 눈을 뜨고 일어났습니다.

"흥부야, 내가 잘못했다."

놀부는 눈물을 흘리며 뉘우쳤습니다.

"형님, 우리 집으로 가서 함께 살아요."

그 뒤로 흥부와 놀부는 마을 사람들이 부러워하는 사이 좋은 형제가 되었습니다.